Exploring
the West

Rosie McCormick

Core Knowledge

ISBN: 978-1-68380-430-7

Exploring the West

Table of Contents

Daniel Boone

As a boy, Daniel Boone made friends with the Lenape, the Native Americans who lived in the forests. They taught him many skills, such as how to walk quietly on wooded paths, how to follow footprints made by animals, and how to hunt.

When he grew up, Daniel Boone and his wife, Rebecca, lived in the forest in North Carolina. They had ten children, and they lived together in a big, one-room log house. Over time, Daniel began to think about moving farther west.

Daniel, like other Americans, had heard about beautiful land in the western part of the United States. At the time, about one million Americans lived up and down the East Coast.

He had heard about new places where they could farm and build towns.

Now Daniel and others wanted to explore these places, but their path was blocked by the Appalachian Mountains.

Daniel set off with friends to find a way through the Appalachian Mountains. The men came upon a Native American path that made it easier for them to make their way.

Native Americans hunted in the Appalachian Mountains and in the forests on the land below. They called this area Kenta-ke, which means "meadowland." Across the mountains, the men saw land for farming and large, leafy forests.

Daniel wondered how he could bring Rebecca, his children, and everything else he owned to this new land. There was no road through the Appalachian Mountains. It would be difficult for wagons to cross the mountains without a clear path. Daniel knew he needed a wide, flat road that would take them into Kentucky.

Daniel and other men set to work to clear a way through. They cut down tall trees. They worked day and night. The path they cleared was called the Wilderness Road.

The Wilderness Road ended at the Kentucky River, where Daniel Boone and the men built a fort. Daniel named it Fort Boonesboro.

The Wilderness Road was the only road through the mountains to Kentucky. Thousands of people followed the Wilderness Road across the mountains. They traveled with wagons filled with almost everything they owned and their heads filled with dreams. They wanted to go west.

The Louisiana Purchase

Imagine you live with your father, your mother, and your two sisters in a wooden cabin that looks like a small box. Inside the cabin are all the things your family owns. Every morning, you look outside and see that you are surrounded by deep, rolling water. Your home is a house on a boat—a flatboat—that floats in the Mississippi River.

You stand on top of the cabin. You steer the boat with long oars. You drift down the mighty Mississippi River, one of the few ways to reach the West. But you are heading south to the busy city of New Orleans, which will be your new home.

At night, under the light of a glowing lantern, you write down your thoughts and dreams.

As you get closer to New Orleans, you see boats carrying barrels of apples, salt, bags of flour, tobacco, and wood. These are things Americans trade with one another and with other countries.

Boats constantly stop at the noisy port of New Orleans to load and unload. The port is where traders send goods to other states and across the Atlantic Ocean to Europe. But there is a problem. New Orleans is not an American city. It belongs to France.

The United States owns most of the land from the Atlantic Ocean to the Mississippi River. But if you cross the Mississippi, you are standing on land owned by another country—France. France owns all the land west to the Rocky Mountains. That huge area is called Louisiana and is about as big as the United States at this time.

President Thomas Jefferson wants to buy this land from France. He wants American farmers to more easily use the port of New Orleans. He has written a letter to the French government, and he has sent two men to France to try to buy New Orleans.

The ruler of France at this time is Napoleon Bonaparte. Napoleon wants to be the greatest leader in the world. He wants France to be the most powerful country in the world. He is leading France in a war against Great Britain.

At first, Napoleon says he will not sell any land. But he needs lots of money to fight the war against Great Britain. So he changes his mind and says the United States can buy New Orleans and *all* of Louisiana for $15 million. This may sound like a lot of money, but it is a very low price for all that land.

The two men sent to France by President Jefferson say yes to the deal, which is called the Louisiana Purchase. President Jefferson hears the good news on the night before the Fourth of July. Soon after, America takes control of New Orleans.

Lewis and Clark

Many people, including President Jefferson, were curious to find out what was out there in the Louisiana Territory. How big was it? Who were the Native Americans living there? Was there a river that went all the way across the Louisiana Territory to the Pacific Ocean? President Jefferson decided to send two men, Meriwether Lewis and William Clark, to explore this land.

Meriwether Lewis was an army leader who knew how to live outdoors. William Clark had also been a soldier. He had explored frontier lands and was a talented artist.

Lewis and Clark led a group of about forty men. They called themselves the Corps of Discovery. The Corps started their journey by traveling in two large canoes on the Missouri River. One of the canoes carried tents, tools, clothing, guns, and food.

The Corps brought such things as hatchets and mirrors to trade with Native Americans. Their horses walked ahead on the banks of the river. Lewis's dog also traveled with the group.

The summer sun blazed down on the men. Heavy rains soaked them. Mosquitoes bit them. They saw animals they had never seen before—antelope, white pelicans, and prairie dogs. Lewis called prairie dogs "barking squirrels." But when winter came, the men had to stop. Rivers froze over.

The men built a fortlike shelter to protect themselves from the bitter cold. The Mandan people, who lived nearby, visited them, telling stories about the great Rocky Mountains ahead. The Mandan had long traded with and helped trappers involved in the fur trade.

When the warm breezes of spring came, the Corps began their trip again. A young Shoshone woman named Sacagawea went along as a guide. She knew the land ahead, and she could speak several Native American languages. Sacagawea's husband, Charbonneau, and her baby, Jean Baptiste, went along too. The Corps called the baby Little Pomp!

As the Corps traveled west, the rivers they journeyed along got smaller. Finally, the rivers ended. Up ahead were the mighty Rocky Mountains, which blocked the way west. The men and Sacagawea would have to climb over them.

When winter came again, the snow made the journey almost impossible. The explorers were wet and cold and half-starved. They could not find animals to hunt. The Corps melted snow for drinking water and ate candles, which were made of animal fat.

The Corps traveled across the Rocky Mountains for three and a half months. Finally, the explorers came upon the Columbia River.

They followed this river all the way until they stood on the shores of the Pacific Ocean. Against all odds, they had succeeded!

Sacagawea

You have already met Sacagawea. But there is much more to her story. When Sacagawea was ten years old, she was captured and taken far away from her home by the Hidatsa, a Native American people.

When she was older, Sacagawea married Charbonneau, a French Canadian. Together, they hunted animals and traded furs. When they met Meriwether Lewis and William Clark, they joined the Corps.

One day, both Lewis and Clark walked along the edge of the river. A sudden wind struck the canoe that carried all their papers, books, tools, medicines, and everything else they owned.

Charbonneau was in the canoe, but he didn't know how to swim. He accidentally turned the canoe over on its side, dumping everything into the river. Sacagawea jumped into the river and saved all the things that had washed overboard.

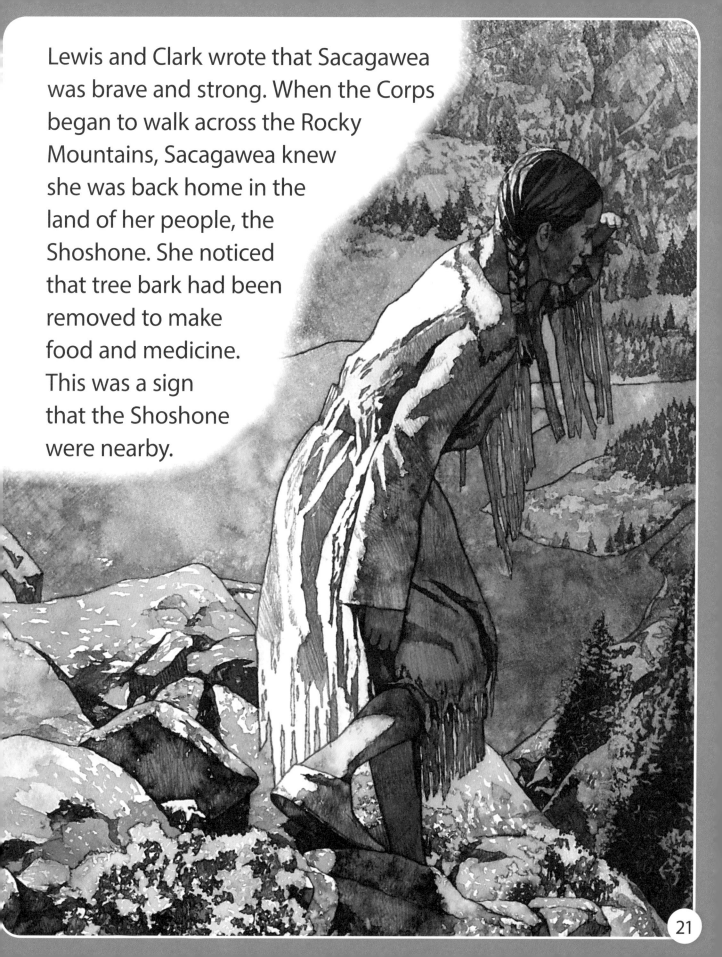

Lewis and Clark wrote that Sacagawea was brave and strong. When the Corps began to walk across the Rocky Mountains, Sacagawea knew she was back home in the land of her people, the Shoshone. She noticed that tree bark had been removed to make food and medicine. This was a sign that the Shoshone were nearby.

The Corps needed horses to carry all their belongings across the Rocky Mountains. The explorers needed to trade some of the things they had brought for horses. When they met the Shoshone chief, Sacagawea gasped.

The chief was her long-lost brother! She had found her family again. Her brother agreed to trade horses to Lewis and Clark and to send guides to show them the way across the mountains.

Sacagawea also helped the Corps cross the dangerous, snow-covered Rocky Mountains. When the Corps ran low on food, she knew which berries and roots to eat. Sacagawea helped keep the men alive. Without her, it is unlikely that Lewis and Clark would have made it to the Pacific Ocean.

Sacagawea was a strong, brave woman. We have named mountains and rivers after her. There are statues of her all over our country. Two hundred years later, people still remember her. The United States has made a dollar coin that shows her picture.

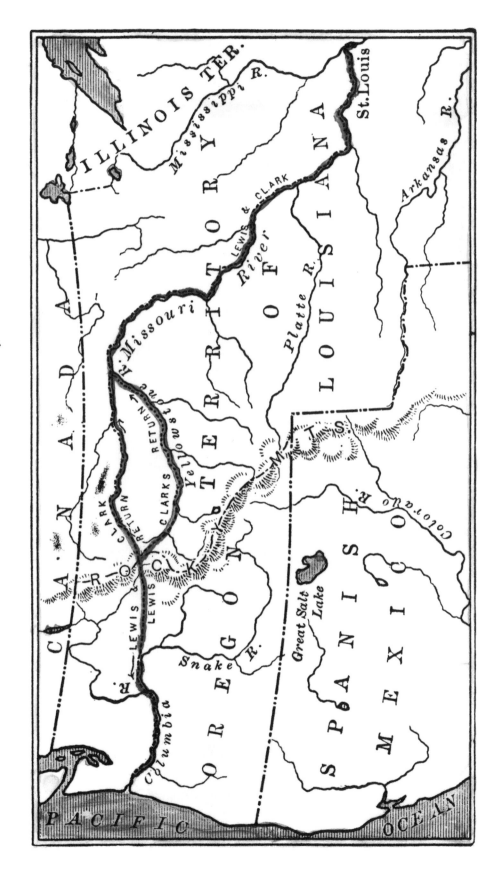

Lewis and Clark's Journey West

Core Knowledge®

CKHG™

Core Knowledge HISTORY AND GEOGRAPHY™

Editorial Directors

Linda Bevilacqua and Rosie McCormick

Subject Matter Expert

J. Chris Arndt, PhD, Department of History, James Madison University

Illustration and Photo Credits